Banffshire's Railways
in photographs by ENC Haywood

Banff Station, 1956.

© Stenlake Publishing, ENC Haywood, 2024
First published in the United Kingdom, 2024,
by Stenlake Publishing Ltd.
54-58 Mill Square,
Catrine, KA5 6RD
www.stenlake.co.uk
ISBN 978-1-84033-974-1

The publishers regret that they cannot supply
copies of any pictures featured in this book.

Printed by
P2D Books, 1 Newlands Rd, Westoning, Bedford MK45 5LD

Interior of Craigellachie North Signal Box, April 1968.

Introduction

Early railway proposals for Banffshire were mostly concerned with finding a route for a railway between Aberdeen and Inverness. However, in July 1845 a prospectus was published for the Banffshire Railway. From Dufftown the railway would have headed north to Keith and Fochabers before reaching its coastal terminus at Portgordon. Initially it looked promising but was dissolved after failing to secure funding, as a result of the financial crisis caused by the Railway Mania. Once again the main schemes were for lines to cross the county. Two main options prevailed. The Aberdeen, Banff and Elgin Railway promoted a line that would follow the coast and River Deveron. The Great North of Scotland Railway's proposal headed inland to use the broad valley of Strath Isla. In the end the inland route was chosen and the Great North of Scotland Railway was granted approval.

In 1854 they opened their line from Kittybrewster in Aberdeen to Huntly. Two years later the line was in Strath Isla and open to Keith. But there its ambitions were thwarted by the Inverness and Aberdeen Junction Railway which reached the town from the west in 1858.

With a through route across the county complete local interests were encouraged. The Banff, Portsoy and Strathisla Railway, with its headquarters in Banff, was promoted by local landowners and businessmen, and approved by Parliament in 1857. They initially ran their own locomotives but the line was not a financial success and in 1863 the Great North of Scotland took over running services for 60% of the receipts. Despite these difficulties the management of the Banff, Portsoy and Strathisla Railway renamed their line the Banffshire Railway and received authorisation to extend from Portsoy to Portgordon. It was never built by them, and in 1867 the Banffshire Railway became part of the Great North of Scotland, the Act enabling the takeover also allowing the Portgordon line to be abandoned.

South of Keith local plans for a line to Dufftown were developed, and approved, but struggled to raise funds for construction. The Great North of Scotland, sensing an opportunity to promote a railway that would link to Elgin, stepped in. They invested in the line and its proposed southern extension along the Spey to Boat of Garten, and built a bridge across the river at Craigellachie to connect to the Elgin-based Morayshire Railway.

Finally after being passed over for decades, the prospect of a Banffshire Coast railway was revived. The Great North of Scotland proposed a line from Portsoy to Buckie in 1881, but in the face of opposition from the Highland Railway (successor to the Inverness and Aberdeen Junction Railway) it was rejected. The following year they resubmitted their plan but this time extending the line to Elgin. At the same time the Highland Railway proposed a line cross country from Keith to Buckie and Portessie. Both lines were approved, and in 1884 the Highland Railway reached Buckie. Two years later the Great North of Scotland opened their Buckie Station on the newly completed coast line.

ENC Haywood journeyed on and photographed Banffshire's railways while visiting relatives in Aberdeen. He loved trains and would take somewhat circuitous routes from his home in Nottingham on his visits north, occasionally passing over the Speyside line and on to Aberdeen, sometimes breaking his journey to travel on a branch line and shortly before its closure photographing the coastal line, a trip he made by car. Included among these Banffshire photographs are a few not in the county, such as Cairnie Junction, in Aberdeenshire (just), because it was the exchange station for the Moray Coast Line. Similarly, although in Morayshire, the Coast Line's impressive Spey Viaduct makes an appearance as the link that saw its approval.

Craigellachie looking east towards Keith Junction. The wagons are sitting on the Speyside Railway side of the station, April 1968.

Station buildings on the Speyside Railway platform of Craigellachie, April 1968.

Overbridge at Craigellachie looking towards Elgin, April 1968.

Towiemore Halt, April 1968.

Bridge carrying Regent Street over the railway in Keith, April 1968.

Keith Town Station from the bridge, April 1968.

Train approaching Keith Junction from Keith Town, April 1968.

The platform for Craigellachie and Keith Town at Keith Junction, April 1968.

Through Aberdeen to Inverness platform at Keith Junction looking west towards Inverness. The goods shed is on the left, April 1964.

Keith Junction looking east, April 1964, the engine shed is on the right of the photograph. There were four platforms at Keith Junction, one through platform for each of the Inverness – Aberdeen and Speyside lines plus two bay platforms. Perhaps surprisingly, when the station was rebuilt in 1988 the opportunity wasn't grasped to provide a second platform for Inverness to Aberdeen trains.

Grange Station, April 1968, looking west to Keith. The station stood at the western end of a triangular junction for the Moray Coast Line and Banff Branch.

Grange Station looking west. On the right is the bay platform where services to Banff once terminated. April 1968.

At the triangular junction's eastern side was Cairnie Junction, photographed April 1968. It didn't serve a local community but was instead an interchange station allowing passengers to change trains to or from direct Aberdeen to Inverness services with those using the Moray Coast Line.

Cairnie Junction, 1956. The spur leading to the Moray Coast Line was constructed in 1886, but the station wasn't opened until 1898 when the line from Rothiemay to Keith was doubled.

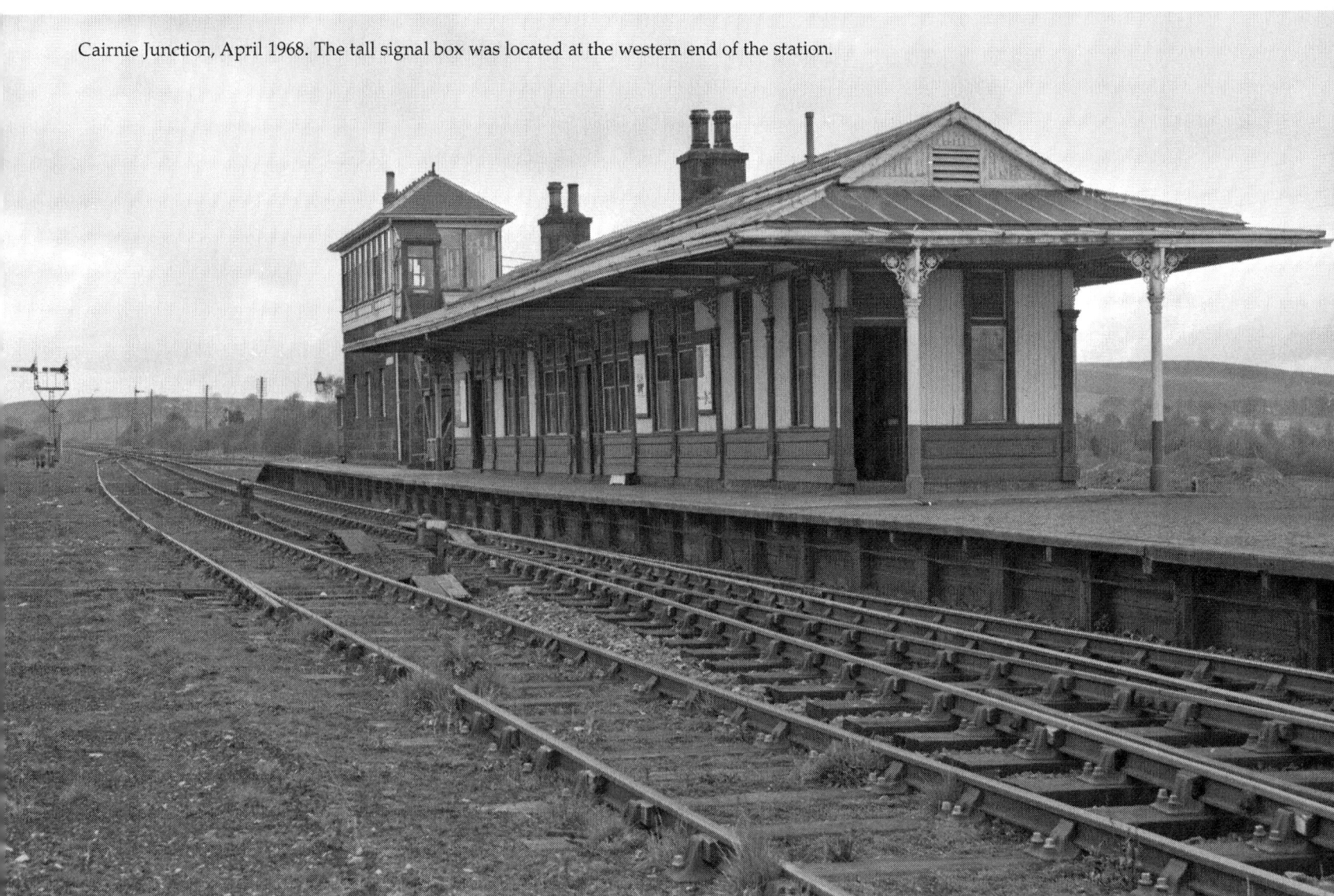
Cairnie Junction, April 1968. The tall signal box was located at the western end of the station.

Cairnie Junction, April 1968, shortly before the station closed. Once the Moray Coast Line was cut the station no longer served any purpose.

Looking west from the signal box at Cairnie Junction, April 1968. The Moray Coast Line curves right while the line to Inverness continues into the distance.

There was no station on the northern corner of the triangular junction only Grange North Signal Box. Photographed, April 1968, looking towards Banff from a train that has left Cairnie Junction.

Knock Station, April 1968. The ballast still bears the scars of the now lifted loop line through the station, but there is no trace of the other platform that once stood alongside it. Knockdhu Distillery is in the background on the east side of the station with a siding leading to it.

Glenbarry looking south towards Grange, April 1968. The track here is also being lifted but the removal of the disused platform and overbridge hasn't advanced to the state at Knock.

Tillynaught looking south towrds Grange, April 1964. Opened in 1859, at the junction between the Banff, Portsoy and Strathisla Railway's lines to the two coastal towns.

The Banff platform at Tillynaught, April 1964.

Station signs at Tillynaught, April 1964.

Tillynaught Banff Platform looking north towards Banff, July 1962.

Bridgefoot Halt, July 1962, looking towards Banff.

No. 79054 with the train from Banff approaching Bridgefoot Halt, July 1962.

Golf Club House Halt, July 1962. Both it and Bridgefoot Halt were opened in 1913.

Banff Station, 1956.

The cramped terminus at Banff, April 1964.

Goods yard and shed, Banff, April 1964.

The Moray Coast Line Platforms at Tillynaught looking towards Portsoy, 1956.

Viewed from the end of the Elgin and Coast platform the Portsoy Branch side of Tillynaught Station, 1956.

Portsoy Station, August 1960, looking towards Buckie. This was the replacement station opened in 1884. The original terminus station was bypassed to create the through route along the Moray Coast, and was sited off the right-hand side of this photograph.

Tochieneal Station looking west with the infrastructure being dismantled in preparation for the line's closure. April 1968.

Cullen Station, April 1968.

The viaduct to the west of Cullen at Seatown, June 1960.

Portknockie looking west, April 1968.

Portknockie looking east, April 1968.

Findochty Station looking east, June 1960.

Findochty looking west, April 1968.

Portessie signal box at the east end of the station, April 1968.

Portessie Station looking west, April 1968. The morass on the left lies beside the platform of the Highland Railway's line from Keith to Buckie and Portessie.

Buckie Station, 1956.

Exterior Buckie Station, 1956.

Buckie Station looking west, 1956.